Linked
in
Prayer

This book of prayers was written by members of the
Association of Anglican Women in New Zealand,
for Christian Family Year,
to celebrate our beginnings
in the centennial of the
Senior Fellowship at Avonside, Christchurch,
the first Mothers' Union formed in New Zealand

Linked in Prayer

Everyday Prayers for Everyday People

Rosemary Atkins
Dorothy Brooker
Rosalind Buddo
Philippa Chambers
Audrey England
Alice White

COLLINS

The Authors warmly thank those young people who wrote the prayers in Chapter 3 and also a number of other contributors who wrote out of their experience or in their special generation.

Two prayers, Trusting Teenagers and Will I Still Know my Husband, are reprinted by permission from PRAYERS FROM A MOTHER'S HEART by Judith Mattison, Copyright Augsburg Publishing House and Mayhew McCrimmon Ltd.

Collins Liturgical Publications
8 Grafton Street, London W1X 3LA

Available in New Zealand from
Collins Publishers, PO Box 1, Auckland

Distributed in Ireland by
Educational Company of Ireland
21 Talbot Street, Dublin 1

Collins Liturgical Australia
PO Box 316, Blackburn, Victoria 3130

First published in New Zealand in 1986
by the Association of Anglican Women

Expanded edition, first published by Collins, 1987

Copyright © text and illustrations 1986 and 1987, Rosemary Atkins

ISBN 0 00 599996 0

Printed by William Collins Sons & Co, Glasgow

CONTENTS

YOUNG PEOPLE

THOSE SPECIAL PEOPLE

CELEBRATIONS

PERSONAL

TIMES OF NEED

THANK YOU

NIGHT AND DAY

Preface

I am both delighted and honoured to have been asked to commend this book of family prayers, which has been compiled to mark the centenary in 1986 of the founding of the Mothers' Union in New Zealand.

The Mothers' Union is now part of the Association of Anglican Women in New Zealand. Both our organisations seek to sustain and uphold Christian family life. This book of prayers has been written mainly by members of the Association of Anglican Women for Christian Family Year, as they designated their centenary year.

Both the A.A.W. and the Mothers' Union help families to 'locate their spirituality in everyday life'. These realistic and very personal prayers, which cover many of the ups and downs of family life, will I am sure help children, young people and adults as they experience different concerns, worries and joys in their journey through life. I can think of no better way of marking this milestone in the life of the church in New Zealand than this book of contemporary prayers, some written by young people, which deal with the realities of modern family life as they experience it.

Many families, including Christian families, in all parts of the world are today facing great pressures and need to be able in a relevant way to share their hopes and joys with the God of love, who is the same yesterday, today and forever.

I am sure this book of prayers which covers so many facets of family life and which has been produced with great imagination and love will fulfil a great personal need in the prayer life of many families. I am full of admiration for the women of New Zealand A.A.W. who have contributed to it.

Hazel Treadgold
Central President, The Mothers' Union

Our Family

Teach us to love

Father of us all,
    accept our thanks for the joys of family life.
Help us to live so that we can strengthen and enrich this life.
May our family welcome with you,
      the stranger,
      the lonely
      and the needy.
Teach us to love the family of all mankind
    and to realise our part in it;
in the name of Jesus Christ, we ask this.

Lord be in our home

Lord be in our home
    make it yours in every way.

Our thoughts are not always your thoughts,
    constantly we turn from you.
May your love entirely fill this home
    and overwhelm all darkness with your light.

We are your servants,
    make this home your servant too
    so our comfort may be shared with others.

May your spirit always rest here;
    keep our lives on your higher way.
May we see your standards clearly,
    not obscured by wordly views.

Thank you for our home,
    this nest where your love may be nurtured;
    that here it may expand and spread
    out into the world again.

Thank you for this new child

We thank you, God,
   for this new child of your creation.
May the knowledge of you dawn on *her*,
   the love of you grow in *her*,
   and the word of your spirit be seen in *her* life;
through Jesus Christ our Lord.

Each child is different

God, it is so easy to make comparisons
   and yet I know that each of my children is unique.
I will always give thanks
   that each one brings something special to you.
Keep my eyes open to their particular gifts,
   especially the gifts of the one
   who is overshadowed by another.
May they see the love and acceptance I have for them,
   that as a family together
   we will all grow in love for you
   and for each other.

A mother's prayer

Creator God I thank you for the privilege
   of bringing children into this world
   and for the gift of new life.
Give me your guidance,
      your love
      your strength
   as each new day I share with you
   the nurturing and care of my family.
May they grow in stature and in knowledge of you
   filled with your wisdom and your joy for living.

I am called father

You understand, my God,
   what it means to be called Father.
Abba, Dad,
   was on the lips of your child, Jesus.
Father – that word of trust,
       that response of affection,
       that call for strength.
Holy Spirit make my hand firm to hold onto another's,
            my heart warm to give love,
             my guidance clear through word and
               example.
God the Father of my Lord Jesus Christ,
   make me worthy of my calling to be a true Father.

A reconstructed family

Thank you loving God for this home of ours,
   where we nurture our own and each other's children
   of previous unions.
Grant us the special sensitivity we need
   toward each other and the children.
Help us to remember that all families
   have rough times as well as smooth.
By the power of the Holy Spirit
   may we know your wisdom,
          your love,
          your patience,
          your strength,
          your joy,
   that our children may grow together in love
   for you and for each other throughout their lives.
And now we name each of them ....
.... bringing them into the love of Jesus.

A new pattern — adoptive families

Creator God, giver of all life,
   bless those who have given birth to children
   and had the courage to give them to others
   to care for them and bring them up as their own.
We do not know or understand the pain it has been to them.
Bless those who love and bring up these children as a family.
Be with the children in the concerns they have about their heritage.
May we offer love, support and friendship
   to all families we meet in the name of Jesus Christ.

God who is love,
   be with all adoptive families;
Lord who is courage,
   walk with each of them;
Spirit who is peace,
   lead them on and enfold them
   in your loving peace, now and always.

I may never hear *him* acknowledge you

Dear God and Father of us all
      . . . . does not accept you
    or the redemptive work of your Son, Jesus Christ.
But I believe that the love we have for each other
    is a love which, in the sacrament of marriage,
      has been blessed by you.
We are together, enfolded in your love.
I believe that in loving *him* and giving of myself
    I am giving you.
I believe that in loving me and our children
    he encounters love and you are love.
I may never live to hear *him* acknowledge you
    as creator, redeemer, friend,
      but in love and trust
      I continue to surrender *him* to your boundless mercy
      with praise and thanksgiving.

Still me when I panic . . . a solo parent prays

God who makes creation,
    God who stills storms,
Move me when I stagnate,
    Still me when I panic.
Still me now with the stillness that refreshes and brings new life.
. . . (Be still, become quietly aware of breathing,
    and let go of anxieties one by one) . . .

Thank you for the times of nurture and warmth
    with children within my care.
. . . (Remember specific times) . . .
God may your Spirit nurture me, with them.

Thank you for my ability to work and strive among my peers
. . . (Recall some of your strengths and skills) . . .
God may your Spirit strengthen me
    that I may bear my responsibility in the work place.

Thank you for the extension of myself in so many ways,
  father, colleague, home maker.
. . . (Recall specific times) . . .
God may your spirit so direct me that when I feel
    over-stretched,
    hurt,
    alone,
I may find the direction and power you offer all creation
  to be whole, to find myself.

For the special person in the family

Loving God, thank you for the Spirit
  that has enabled . . . . to lead as normal a life as possible,
  and for the others in the family who have encouraged this.
Thank you for those who care for the disabled,
  whether physically, mentally or emotionally.
Thank you for their love, understanding and vision
  that brings healing, comfort and peace to those in their care.
Inspire those who are insensitive to the needs of others
  to become more fully aware of their problems and difficulties;
  may they express their concern in such a way
  that the dignity and independence of each person is enriched;
  in the name of him whose love enriches us all, Jesus Christ.

Now that . . . . is leaving home

Lord, grant that our home is a secure place,
  warm, loving and welcoming,
  always good to return to.
Now that . . . . is leaving home
  we ask you to surround *her* with your protection and guidance.
We have had the early years to influence and teach by our example,
  and now we entrust . . . . . . to your care as *she* goes out into the world.
Bless *her* and give *her* the strength *she* will need
  and the knowledge that you are always with *her*
  through the grace of our Lord Jesus Christ.

Trusting teenagers

Jesus, it is very hard to allow children to grow up.
We focus on them for so long
    that it is painful to watch them make mistakes
    as they break free on their own.
It is difficult to admit that sometimes
    they make better decisions for themselves
    than we would make for them.
It is hard not to be in control.
Now our child chooses not to attend church.
I wrestle with making an issue of it, Lord.
If I become too forceful,
    will the meaning of the services be lost
    in resentment at being forced to attend?
If I do not occasionally insist on my values,
    will my values be lost from my children?
    Or can I trust, Lord?
Help me trust them.
Give me trust that our family atmosphere
    and years of value-teaching will not be lost
    in these searching years.
Let me trust that my children are capable
    of making intelligent decisions about
    whatever confronts them –
    drugs, church, friends, careers, elections.
Help me remember that occasional misjudgments
    did not ruin, but often strengthened my understanding of life.
Help me see the truth in the ideas that we learn best by doing,
    that different kinds of experiences can be equally meaningful to lives.
Let me trust them and believe that you do not forsake them,
    but continue to seek
    all of us in every event of life.
You watch them
    and you watch us. Bless us, Lord.

I'm always coming and going from home

Between the fond farewell and the welcome embrace,
  my feet travel but my heart stays home.
Divine Spirit, whose presence is everywhere,
  keep us in our comings and goings.
Divine Protector, keep me safe when I journey
  and guard my family at home.
  Let no distance separate us but bonds of affection bind us
  until I return again.
Divine Redeemer, may these frequent excursions
  prepare me without fear for the partings of life;
  let me see in them signs of resurrection
  and hope for my final going and coming home.

The house is so empty

Loving God,
  the house is so empty tonight
  and yet I know it is filled with your presence.
Help me to accept that I will not know
  the love of a family of my own,
  nor experience the daily joys, concerns and sorrows
  of a growing family.
Yet Lord, I do thank you for the great joy
  of sharing the love of many families,
  and the outstretched arms of children
  who greet me with love in their eyes.
Thank you for the gift of true friends with whom I can relax
  and with whom I do not have to pretend.
  May we together share one another's burdens;
  I need them to be loving listeners and helping hands.
Help me also to be loving and caring.
May I use my interests of *music, gardening, art, countryside*
  to fill the empty spaces and to restore my spirit.
Lord this evening the telephone did not ring;
  help me to realise that I too must remember
  that a few words of mine can lift a burden
  and inspire new hope for others.
I ask this in Jesus' name.

Our young people

Giver of all life, we pray
    that as the young people in each new generation
    discover your world in their own way,
    their energies may be used creatively in your service,
    and their choices based on what is true and of real value;
    we ask it in the name and for the honour of Jesus Christ our Saviour.

Our family – finding real love

Lord Jesus,
    you knew the life of an earthly home,
    the joys and the concerns it can bring.
Help our family to know real love for one another;
    love that shows endearment,
    love that cares and is concerned for others,
    love that is sensitive to the needs that we often find hard
    to put into words.
Bless O Lord, our giving and sharing,
                our loving and living
    and may we know your presence always with us.

Accepting the changing situation

O God, as you accept each one of us,
    grant us the grace to accept the decisions
    that some in our family have made.
Help us to be supportive and loving, and to remember
    that all things work together for good to them that love God.
Guide and bless
    those whose lives are most affected by this change
    and bring us all closer to you;
    through Jesus Christ.

Will I still know my husband?

Sometimes mothers become buffers.
   We try to help fathers understand why
   teenage sons want long hair.
We attempt to demonstrate to children
   the respect and understanding their fathers need.
Lord, give me direction or I will become
   a peacemaker with no identity or conviction –
   absorbing conflicts like paper towels,
   and smoothing rough waters.
I must look ahead.
Five, ten, fifteen years from now,
   I will be less a buffer and more a wife.
My husband must be my primary relationship.
   It's so hard Lord, because children,
   and smoothing and interpreting take so much time.
Often husbands get less time.
Sometimes we think of husbands as fathers
   more than as mates.
When I am living in a home empty of children,
   will I still know my husband –
   will I know who he is?
Help me realise that
   even though my husband does not grow taller
   he is still growing –
   he needs change, too.
Help me to seek to know him
   as much as I observe and acknowledge
   the growing and changing of my children.
Let me not get so involved in mediation
   that I lose sight of the relationship
   on which this family was initially built.
My marriage will outlive my mothering role.

Our child is sick

God of all,
  in the sure knowledge of your
    infinite love for each of us;
  may we know your peace,
    your strength,
    your nearness to us now.
Creator and sustainer of life
  surround with your healing power
  . . . in *her* sickness.
  In *her* weakness and pain
    bring to *her* those whose skill and caring
    can give comfort and healing.
  As we watch and wait,
    empower us to cope with our own feelings
    of inadequacy and uncertainty.
We surrender . . . to your care.
Give us now your peace and your love.

I sense their helplessness as they stand and watch

God of us all,
  I am in your loving care,
    supported by your healing power
    and the prayers of my family and friends.
  I am secure in the knowledge
    that all around me are people who are trained
    and they can cope if any emergency happens.
  But I see the uncertainty and the fear of the unknown
    in the eyes of my family as they come and visit —
  I sense their helplessness as they stand and watch.
God, help them to be aware of your love which surrounds them.
  May they see your hand in the hands of those who care for me.
  May we know your presence with us all.

I think *she's* sleeping with *her boyfriend*

Dear God, I think . . . is sleeping with *her boyfriend.*
  It feels as if everything I have believed in
    and valued has been shattered.
  And if *she's* sleeping with this *boyfriend,*
    what happens if the relationship ends?
Will *she* sleep with the next one?
Is this a repudiation of all my values?
She must know what I feel about sex before marriage.
Why Lord?
But it is *her* life;
  I cannot live it for *her.*
  She must make *her* own decisions.
  All I can do, and all you would want me to do,
    is to love *her* and to continue
      to surrender *her* to your loving guidance.
  I give *her* to you in Jesus' name.

If we fail

Loving God, we ask you to be with us in our homes.
Guide us as parents
  in what we do in difficult times.
If we fail, show us your love and grace;
  give us strength to try again.
May we find encouragement
  from other christian families and from you;
  through your Son, Jesus Christ, our Lord.

A grace

Bless this feast, Lord God,
  and nourish us with your goodness
  every day of our lives,
  through Jesus Christ our Lord.

A handful of prayers
(origin unknown)

My thumb is nearest to me,
   so I remember to pray
      for my nearest and dearest
      . . . (family and friends) . . .

Next comes my index finger,
   the one my teacher wags at me;
      with this I remember to pray
      for teachers and schools,
      for clergy, church and missionaries.

The middle finger is my longest finger;
   it reminds me to pray for those in authority:
      for church leaders,
      prime ministers and governments,
      and anyone given responsibility
      to make decisions which affect others.

The next finger is the weakest on my hand
   so I pray specially
      for anyone who is sick
      or lonely
      or in need of any sort.

Finally
   with my little finger
      I pray for my own needs.

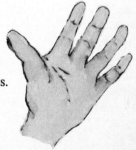

For my family

Thank you Lord
    for my family who love me.
Help me to be loving too
    and to show them that I care.
Bless us all ....
    and keep us in your care.

Thank you for my grandparents

Thank you God
    for my grandparents;
    they are very special people.
Bless them
    and take care of them always.

For my godparents

Dear Lord,
    today I specially remember my godparents.
Bless them and their families
    now and always.

Arguing

Please God stop them!
I hate it when they argue;
   they say awful things to each other.
Help them to hear what they are saying;
   calm them down so they stop hurting each other
   and help them to say they're sorry.
Please Jesus
   shine your light of love
   on .... and .... right now.

My dad's not here

Dear God,
   bless my Dad today,
   wherever he is.

For the people who work at night

Bless those people, Lord,
   who stay awake to work
   whilst we are asleep;
   the policemen and the firemen,
   those who look after people who are ill,
   the pilots of planes,
   the drivers of buses and trains,
   those whose work we do not know.
Keep them safe from all danger
   and watch over them in their loneliness;
   through Jesus Christ our Lord.

I'm sorry God

I'm sorry God,
    for anything I've said
                or done
                or thought today
    which has hurt anyone,
    especially those I care about most.
Help me to be a good friend,
    willing to share and understand.
Thank you for always forgiving us
    when we say we're sorry.

I have so much to thank you for

Loving Father,
    I have so much to thank you for;
        for my healthy body,
        for eyes to see,
        for ears to hear;
        for my comfortable home,
        for a family who love me;
        for friends and the good times we have together;
        for fun and laughter and for this beautiful country
        and for ....
I thank you for all these things
    and ask you to help me
    never to take them for granted.

Thank you for creation

Dear God,
    thank you for your creation;
    thank you for the birds and the butterflies,
        for the flowers in the garden which give us joy;
    thank you for the tall trees in the forest,
        and for the fields that grow food for us to eat;
    thank you for the stars that guide us,
        and for the sun which gives us light
        and keeps us warm.

Help me to laugh and sing again

Thank you Father God
    for knowing how I feel
    and for being with me now when I'm sick.
Stay close to me, I pray,
    and let me know your love.
Help me to get better,
    to laugh and sing again,
    and thank you Lord for everyone
    who's looking after me.

Angels

God of all creation,
    send your guardian angels
    to watch over .... and ....
    while they sleep.
Guard them
    from all nightly fears and fantasies.
May they sleep in peace,
    in the knowledge of your love
    and in the presence of your Holy Spirit.

Lord be the guest of this house

Lord, be the guest of this house;
    keep far from it all the deceits of the evil one.
    May your holy angels watch over us
    as guardians of our peace;
    and may your blessing be always upon us;
    through Jesus Christ our Lord.

(from Compline)

The light of your love

Lord Jesus,
   sometimes I'm afraid of the dark.
Keep me safe
   from all the things that scare me
   in the night.
Jesus, I ask for the light of your love
   to be all around me
   and on all the people I care about.

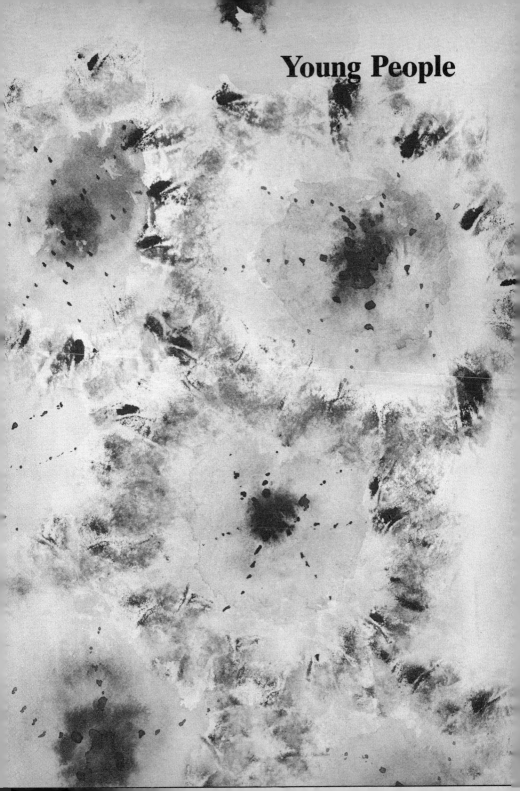

Young People

It's great to be alive and to be young

My God it's great
                to be alive,
                to be young
                to enjoy all that life gives me.
Thank you for my life,
                my health,
                my family,
                my friends.
    Be with me in all I do.

God, who are you?

Dear God,
    who are you?
    How do I know who you are
    or where you are?
    My priest said you are all around
But where?
I don't seem able to feel you
                    or see you
                    or anything.
I suppose I know you're able to hear me,
    I learnt that ages ago;
    but I still find it hard
    not knowing who you are;
    please let me see who I can pray to.
Thank you.

Help me to believe

Help me to believe in you;
            to be faithful to you.
Help me to pass your word on
    without feeling foolish.

I have been a Christian for only a few months

I have been a Christian for only a few months Lord
   and I feel great to be part of your family.
I pray for the thousands who do not know you.
Help me to do what I can in the world
   to show your love.
Thank you for showing me how much you love me
   and want to forgive me;
     through the life and death of Jesus.

It's hard to be a Christian today Lord

It's hard to be a Christian today Lord.
I hear your name taken in vain.
It often seems easier
   to stand back than to be involved,
   to hurt than to help.
Teach me to be brave
   and to know that you are with me.
Help me to share your love and joy.

I'm sorry I hurt you, Lord

Forgiving God,
   I was acting on impulse,
      going along with the crowd.
   Like Saint Peter at your trial
      it was only when I said the words
      that I realised what I had done.
I didn't mean to hurt you
   and I'm really sorry for it now.
I know by your great love for me
   you'll forgive me and forget it
   and go on loving me still.

I'm sorry I missed my deadline

Lord Jesus,
   I'm sorry I missed my deadline
   and let all those people down.
Please give me the chance to make it up to them.
It's just that everything is happening at once.
I can't think straight with all the pressures
   and don't have much spare time.
I am trying.
Please help me.

I have exams today

I have exams today
   and I'm panicking Lord.
   I feel I can't remember a thing.
   I've tried to work.
   I could have done more.
Help me to remember what I have learnt
   and to read the questions properly.
Calm me down Lord,
   and stop me shaking.

Thank you for my new friend

Dear Lord,
   thank you for the way *she* is,
   the way *she* makes me laugh so much.
   I was beginning to wonder if anyone would really like me
     and *she* came along.
   They don't seem to tease me any more
     or is it that I just don't hear them?
   Whatever, the time we spend together is choice.
   I thank you for that time
     and look forward to more.

Thank you for my *boyfriend*

Dear Jesus,
   I want to thank you for my *boyfriend*.
   Thanks for bringing us together at that dance.
   Don't think Mum likes *him*, but Dad does;
      or I think he does.
   Dad teases me about *him*.
      It's good – just like he teased Jane and her boyfriend.
   I like being with *him*,
      the way *he* held my hand in church last week.
   You don't mind do you? Mum'd kill me!!
   My friends say that your first *boyfriend* is the best.
   I wouldn't know, I only want the one.
   I hope *he* prays for me too.

They're picking on me

I think they're all picking on me.
If they don't get off my back
   I'll go round the bend.
They don't bother about me.
They've forgotten that I've got feelings.
Loving Lord,
   let
     them
       give
         me
           space,
   for you know
   how much I need it now.

I feel out of my circle of friends

I feel I am on the outside Lord,
   pushed out of my circle of friends;
   nothing that I do seems to please them any more.
You know how it feels to be like this.
Guide me as I try to find out what's gone wrong
   and help us all to patch up these friendships.

Why do they treat me as a child?

O God,
   why do they treat me as a child?
It's just not fair.
I'm always too young for anything I want to do.
   When will they let me grow up and let me be like my friends?
   They're always allowed to go out when they want.
   I know they are trying to do it for my good,
      but sometimes they're so unfair.
Help us all to change.
Help me to grow up.

They want me to be a . . .

O God, they want me to be a . . . .
I can't think of anything worse.
I think they've forgotten it's my life and not theirs.
I know it's going to hurt them,
   but give me courage and determination
   and the right words Lord to make them see
   that this is what I really want to do.
May we listen to each other with tolerance and understanding,
   so that together we will find an answer.
Give us your strength Lord,
   for I know we're going to need it.

I don't know what I want to be

Heavenly Father,
   I still don't know what I want to be.
   Everybody at school has decided; they did that last year.
   "It's time you made up your mind," they say, "or you won't get a job."
   But I've really got no idea and I don't want to choose.
Why can't they leave me alone?
   I am still looking.
      Have you got something for me?
        I think I'd like that.

What's the point of swotting?

Why should I swot to pass exams?
What's the point!
It all seems so irrelevant —
I'll never use it again!
Why should I bother?
God,
   I know I should be doing my best
      because the ability I have
      comes from you.
   Give me the patience and the will
      to sit down and swot,
      for it is by working
      that your purpose for us is fulfilled.

I still can't find a job

O God, I still can't find a job.
   I'm trying so hard but I don't have the right skills.
   Mum says it won't be long now but John took a whole year.
God I can't wait that long!
   Interviews every week but still nothing.
   People think I'm not trying.
   It's so hard —
   I find it hard to take the dole knowing what they say.
Give me strength.

Teach us to care for our world

Loving and Holy Spirit of God
 teach us to care for the resources of the world,
 to keep the earth beautiful and unpolluted
 and to see that all will have their share.

We pray that we and all people may work together
 to show your kingdom on earth.
May the world learn your way of peace and freedom,
 so that all nations will learn to share with their people
 equal rights and opportunities,
 and that we may all come before you in worship and praise;
 through Jesus Christ our Lord.

I don't want to smoke

I don't want to smoke . . . .
 the others are doing it Lord,
 and the pressure is getting hard for me to join them.
Loving God, you gave me life and health.
Help me to value these gifts to me.
 May I, in the company of friends,
  know a confidence in daily living
  that depends not on drugs,
  but on your love for me.

Youth has many fears, hopes and joys

Merciful God,
    today's youth experience many fears,
    many hopes and joys
    as they grow from children into adults.
We pray that you will guide us along the right path,
    helping us to make the right decisions
    and to cope with our daily lives.

Being young is sometimes very difficult

Dear Lord,
    being young is sometimes very difficult.
    We get told to "grow up"
        but are treated like children.
    There are lots of pressures from friends
        which run against your teaching;
    but Father
        we rejoice in our youth and the opportunities you have given us
        to lead our lives by your Son's example.
We pray that your Holy Spirit may be seen in our lives
    and guide us in all we do.

I think I'm pregnant

I think I'm pregnant!
I'm scared to find out the truth.
I need to tell someone;
I need to know what to do.
Gracious God,
    give me the guidance
    to find someone who will not condemn,
    but who will support me and help me.

He abused my trust

I trusted you and you let me down!
Everyone must know!
Where can I go?
I feel so unclean, so unworthy!
I want to curl up and die!

I must talk to someone!

God, I feel your forgiveness might help —
    but I didn't do anything that was wrong.
    Perhaps I need
        your courage to talk to . . . (minister/priest, teacher, aunt, friend, grandparent)
        your help to know that I can trust them,
        your wisdom to know my worth,
        your strength to work this through.

    Jesus said 'Do not be afraid
                I will be always with you.
                I give my peace to you.'

My parents are divorced

Dear God,
    I was born out of their love
    and find the hurt of their separation
    often too hard to bear.
Jesus Christ,
    you know about pain,
    so you know how I feel.
    Their decisions have been made.
Help me now to accept each parent
    and to accept myself.
Please may love and friendship grow
    as we relate again to each other
    and to you.

He didn't deserve to lose his job!

Oh God, I'm so worried about Dad.
I'm angry too — he didn't deserve to lose his job!
He's always worked hard and been conscientious,
    and now he's been laid off.
I wish he would talk about it — but he won't.
I know he lies awake hour after hour at night, worrying
    and I know he feels useless and humiliated.
Sometimes I find it hard not to be irritated with him
    when he doesn't see the things that need doing around here.

Please God, give me the patience to understand
    and support him in his struggles.
    Help him to realise that we don't depend on his income
        in order to love and respect him.
    Help the rest of the family to be sensitive to his moods
        without wounding his pride.
    I pray that he will find a new role in his life,
        new interests and the will to use this extra time creatively.

Why?
some thoughts

Why don't they want them?
A child of your own blood is a part of you I think;
            but that's just me.
Why do people tangle themselves up in hopeless situations?
Do they think about other people or just about themselves?
Consequences! That's what they don't think about.
I think they should –
            but that's just me.
We have a responsibility to the life we create.
People just think about having a good time, not about tomorrow.
I think they should think about tomorrow,
    the children are tomorrow and tomorrow is theirs.
That's what I think
            but that's just me.
Does anybody think like me?

Those Special People

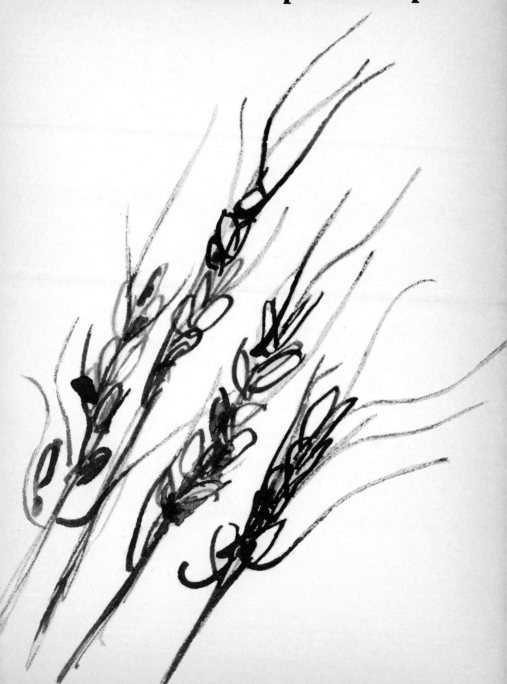

Help me to teach them — a father prays

Heavenly Father, thank you for the children
  who have brought me such joy and happiness.
May your covering wings guard them
  from danger and disaster;
May your healing hand recover them
  from the sickness and accident common to us all;
May your guiding hand lead them
  to the wisdom of deciding what to do
  and give them the courage to do it.
Help me to teach them by precept and example
          to know you,
          to fear you
          and to love you.

Keep them in thy loving care — a grandmother prays

O God, thank you for all thy blessings.
Please enter the hearts and lives of my family
  so that they may be helped and guided to do what is right
  and will please thee. Bless them and keep them in thy loving care
  now and always; for the sake of Jesus Christ.

Sharing the joy — a grandfather prays

Jesus our friend and redeemer, by whose guidance all good works do
  proceed, help us as grandfathers to have such an understanding and
  patience with our grandchildren that we can switch on to their wave-
  length and be a part of their lives. May we, with their parents, share the
  joys of their growing. All this we ask in your name O God our universal
  provider.

I pray for my family — a grandparent prays

O God our Father I pray for my family –
  that they may know thee
  as their Father, friend and guide.
Give them strength to do always what is right,
  and grant that they may know thee as the one true God.
I thank thee for the joy and happiness they bring.
Help me not to be too critical
  of what they feel is right for them to do.
I pray that they will always know
  that thou art with them
  in their joys and in their disappointments.
I ask this through the name of Jesus Christ.

I bring you my godchildren

Loving God, I bring to you my godchildren . . . .
My hopes and fears for their future are in your hands.
Show me where I can take my part
  in sharing responsibility for their spiritual growth.
Remind me of the promises I made at their baptism
  and may they and I grow together
  in knowledge and love of you;
  through Jesus Christ.

Help us to share

Creator, Redeemer and Giver of Life,
  thank you for all the blessings
  you have given us in our country.
Help us to do all we can to share what we have
  to help the hungry children of the world.
We pray that those in authority in the world
  may be drawn by your wisdom and love for all humanity
  to satisfy the needs of all people
  from the abundance of food which you have provided for us;
  through Jesus Christ.

May their spirit know your joy
— a handicapped child

Father of all your children,
  we pray for those whose powers are limited
  by affliction of mind and body.
May their spirit know your joy,
  the peace which passes understanding
  and the great assurance of your love.
Give patience and strength to those who care for them.
Be very near to all families who daily
  see the handicaps of one they love
  and grant them the sure knowledge
  that underneath are the everlasting arms.

Be with new mothers

I've watched my friend's tummy grow – a little enviously,
  and now her baby is to be born.
Be in our hospitals Lord, with new mothers
  who hide their fears under masks of appropriate joy.
You understand how scary hospital routines can be,
  and how much stress and anxiety
  can be hidden under a placid smile.
Make hospital staff sensitive to a new mother's difficulties.
Give understanding to those around mother and baby;
  keep the world from encroaching,
    and let them cocoon away
      to bond as you intended.

Thank you for our neighbours

Loving God, thank you for our neighbours;
    may we be sensitive to their needs
    without encroaching on their privacy.
Help us to be forgiving when they irritate us
    and remind us to look for the good in everyone.
Teach us to believe in others,
        to be ready to support when they need us.
Teach us to be courteous, kind.
By your grace and power
    surround them and us with your love.

Celebrations

We celebrate your birth

Lord Jesus Christ,
   you were born into an earthly family;
   help us as we celebrate your birth
   to share in our family
   the gifts you bring us:
   love,
     joy
       and peace.

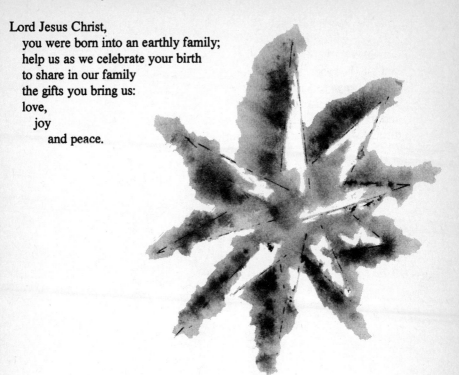

For tuneful carols

Thank you Father,
   for this loved and familiar season,
   for tuneful carols,
   for reunions with families and friends,
   for giving and receiving,
   for a sense of celebration everywhere,
   for all the ways of saying "Christ is born."
We ask that the familiarity of Christmas
   may not smother the truth that we celebrate together.

The wonder of Easter

Eternal God, you gave your Son
  to be our Friend and Saviour.
We thank you that he died for us
  and that he rose again to be with us for evermore.
Help us always to know that he is there
  even when we do not understand,
    and may we know the joy and wonder of the Easter story;
  through Jesus Christ our Saviour.

It was good to ....

Gracious God, we thank you for the happy things
  which happened to us today.
    Especially it was good to ....
Thank you for kindness,
  words of thanks, praise, encouragement;
  for the things which made us feel
  that we were needed and appreciated.
Thank you for new friendships made,
  and for old friends we love.
May we know we are never alone
  and fill us with the joy of your presence.

This special day

Thank you for this time Lord, this special day that seems more sharply
    focused than other days.
We bring you our joy and gladness,
    the offering of a light load and singing hearts.
We want to celebrate more often
    and enjoy the gifts of life with you;
    the holidays, picnics, seasons
    and our children's gifts of love.

Help us to make new memories of celebration,
    stepping aside and holding as precious
    times that slip by without mention.
Help us to build self acceptance in all our family
    by celebrating something unique to each.

Let us remember to celebrate each day,
    to chase depression and aloneness
    with thoughts of charity, love and hope
    so that we may be of use to you.

Preparing for marriage

Loving Father,
    bless those preparing for marriage.
May they learn as they make new discoveries
    and accept new challenges together.
May they be strengthened and enriched
    and grow in their love for each other
    and for you.

Time to enjoy new life together

Merciful God, you gave us to each other
           as man and wife
  and now you have given us time
  to enjoy new life together.
Bless us as we explore
         new tasks,
         new pleasures
         new challenges.
Grant us wisdom, patience, humour and love
  to enrich the years ahead in your strength.

My wife had a baby today

My wife had a baby today!
Boy, oh boy – *no* it's a *girl*
  and I'm glad.
A *daughter,* our child, God's child,
  a new person,
  a gift,
  and a responsibility.
Creator God, bless this child,
  born out of love,
  born into love,
  mine for my wife,
  my darling's for me,
  and ours for our *daughter.*
Keep us true to your love;
  keep us true to our love,
  united together – always.

The gift of a child

Everlasting God, you have blessed .... and .... with the gift of a child.
   May they show their love and thankfulness to you in their home, so that
   by their life and teaching, they may bring up this child in the right way,
   to their own joy, and to your glory.

This amazing experience

This amazing experience,
   the wonder and thrill
   of my new baby's birth.

So perfect.
   Thank you my Lord,
   for this precious life.

Make me worthy of your trust.
Teach me how you would want me
   to care for this new life.
Let me never forget the joy of this time,
   allowing me to share in your creation.

Feeling down? then celebrate

God of all creation
   we come together and rejoice in this celebration.
   We have your love,
            your joy,
            your peace,
            your presence with us.
We acknowledge that we've been through
   times of hardship
   times of questioning
   times of uncertainty.
Thank you for your care and love through these times,
   that today we come with hearts singing
   and hope for the future,
   trusting and knowing you are always with us.
Thank you for each other and the gifts we share.

Personal

Show me how to spend myself — a reflection

This endless list;
Energy spent worrying
    over things best left in your care.
Lord, teach me to leave them there.

When I say "Take my life,"
    I compromise, holding back,
    forgetting your will in my use of time and money,
    allowing my emotions to stampede.

Let me keep hospitality in its rightful place,
    not damaging the fragility of the family.
Teach me to say "No" sometimes;
    "No" to the outside world
    when too much of me is drawn away from home.

Show me how to spend myself;
    make it clear Lord, as my ego doesn't like
    to take the back seat.

My marriage grows stale without time for my husband;
    remind me to stop when he can share time with me.

To spend time with you Lord, is gaining time;
    to listen in stillness
    quietens my mind's chatter
    and brings my priorities back into focus.

Help me to find a balance

Everlasting God help me to find a balance
   in my living day by day.
The church committee (women's group, vestry . . .)
   has asked my help
   and I'd like to be part of your work.
The school committee (floral club, service club . . .)
   has asked me to be leader
   and I'd like to do that too.
You have given me (husband, children, friends and family . . .)
   and they need my help.
   Then there's me – I need time too.
God of infinite wisdom,
   you created our universe in harmony with your love,
   help me each day to balance my living
   that I may share in fulfilling your loving purposes for us all,
   my family, my friends and those who seek my support.

Lord, could you and I get together?

Lord, it would be helpful
   if you and I could get together
   and work out a plan for the future.
I'm not certain where it's taking me
   or what's in store around the corner.
Lord, with you there to help and guide me
   I know I can look at my future with hope
   and plan my life with eagerness and certainty;
   for your name's sake.

I like where I'm at

God I feel great,
 I'm successful,
 I'm popular,
 and I like where I'm at.

I remember Lord,
 the times when life was a struggle,
 the times when my prayers didn't seem to be answered,
 the times when I felt alone and afraid
 and not sure of my own worth.
Thank you for your gifts of strength and perseverance;
 thank you for showing me that I am important to you.
May I never forget that it is through your love
 I am what I am.
Keep me always aware
 of your continual love and patience shown to me;
 through Jesus Christ our Saviour.

Care of my body

I was reminded today, Lord,
 that my body is the temple of the Holy Spirit
 and that I belong to you.

It's so easy to forget
 that to really be myself
 and to work to glorify you
 I have to take care of my health.

Thank you for reminding me to sometimes stop
 and to take stock of my physical self.
Thank you for our doctors and health services,
 for scientists who make life's journey easier.
Gracious God thank you for giving me the strength to cope
 with illness when it does come;
 in your name I pray.

Be near me as I mourn

Lord Jesus Christ, risen and victorious
   I have heard again your words
   of eternal life and of comfort;
   help me to trust them
     as I mourn the death of . . .

   In times of aloneness
           may I know your presence;
   In times of sadness
           may I know your peace;
   In times of uncertainty
           may I know your strength.
   Be with me today and always.

I am sorry

Merciful God as I stand in your light
   I recognise my own weakness.
I thank you for the gift of forgiveness
   when I bring my wrongdoing before you.
I am sorry for the things I have done
   which I know were wrong in your sight.

I am sorry for saying and doing things
   which have hurt others . . . . . .

Lord, I need to be reminded constantly
   to bring my desires and hopes to you
   before I act.
I pray for your gifts of love and wisdom
   to guard my thoughts and tongue before I speak.

I have learned some things today

Eternal God, I have learned some things today
   I never knew before;
I have met people today
   whom I have never met before;
I have thought about some things today
   I have never considered before.
But some things have been allowed to creep in
   that now I am sorry about;
Some things that I fully meant to do,
   I haven't done;
Some words I have spoken hastily
   would have been better unsaid.
Some relationships have been marred by my touchiness.

Forgive me for these things,
   and others, in which I have failed you today
   and fallen far below my best self.

I surrender this day to your mercy and keeping,
   in the sure knowledge that your Holy Spirit
   will refresh and strengthen me
   for the day to come.

May your kingdom come

Gracious God,
   in my acts this day,
   the words I speak
   the thoughts I think
   the tasks I attempt
   the relationships of my daily life;
May your Kingdom come,
   your will be done
   on earth as in Heaven.

Lord, I've been made redundant

Lord, I've been made redundant!
Suddenly I've got no job,
no wages coming in,
no self respect.
The future is about as bleak as it can be!
What am I going to do?
   Please help!
      it's even hard to ask.
Forgive me Lord, but I'm so depressed
  I feel angry,
  unwanted,
  discarded.

I hate interviews with smart young blokes
  who ask those stupid questions;
  most of them don't even bother
    to let me know the outcome.
  Sometimes I wish I were dead.
  My wife and my family get on my nerves.
  I yell at them.

God, help me in these days of searching
    to remember there is a future,
  help me to face my family,
    to support their fears.
I relinquish myself and this whole situation
  into your hands,
  into the freedom that allows you to act.
Thank you for your continuing presence
  that will support us through
    the days ahead.

Times of Need

Making a decision . . .

Dear Lord, you promised
    that where two or three are gathered together in your name,
    you are in the midst of them.
Thank you for your presence with us now.
Guide us as we decide about . . . . . .
May we take no step without you
    and always seek to find your will for us.
        Lead us now and always.

Lord, I am so tired

Jesus, you said,
    "Come to me all who are weary and are heavy laden and I will give you
rest."
I come Lord, tired and dejected.
  But I come
    knowing you will refresh me;
    knowing you will give me strength for another day;
    knowing you will surround me with your love.
I come,
    and leave my burdens at your feet.

I'm fed up

Dear God,
    I'm fed up today,
    I don't know why,
    and it doesn't matter.
I just feel cross
    and bored
    and miserable.
Help me to hold on to your love
    and not take my blackness out on my family.
Be with me until the gloom goes
    and I can feel you there again.

An unplanned baby

Stand Lord,
    with the mother who cannot accept her pregnancy.
Bring to her, people who care.
Help turn her nightmare into life again
    when her decision is made.
May she know inner healing
    and grow to show understanding and compassion for others.

O God, I have found a lump in my breast

O God, I have found a lump in my breast
    and I don't want to know.
My imagination is running riot
    and I'm scared.

Why me Lord?
What have I done to deserve this?
But why not me?

Forgive me Lord, but I panicked!
You are still here
    with all the love, concern and compassion
    I have always claimed and relied upon.
You want for me only that which is the most loving,
    so I trust you to see me through.
I'm still scared,
    but with you I can face the future.

In the name of Jesus Christ,
    touch me with your healing power,
    that power which brings an awareness of your presence
    with all its peace and serenity.
Whatever happens,
    you will be with me,
    giving me the grace and strength to cope.
Thank you Lord for the faith
    you have given me to rely upon you.

Give me patience while my body heals

I feel cooped up in here
    as if I'm tied to this bloody bed.
My friends are all out there,
    fit and free,
    having a great time.

Caring God,
    it's really hard for me
    not to feel sorry for myself
    and be a bag of misery.
Give me patience while my body heals
    and make me less demanding on those who try to care.
Help me to look on the bright side
    and cheer up those around me
    in this sterile ward.

You know the distress of watching loved ones suffer

Thank you Lord for the gifts of this day
    and for my *mother* who welcomes me home
    with a smile of affection
    even when *she* is in pain.
Thank you for *her* silent presence
    when *she* sees me tired and dispirited.

O Loving Father you know the distress
    of watching loved ones suffer.
Thank you for the gentle kindness and patience
    of our district nurses,
    for the work they do,
    the confidence they inspire
    and the encouragement they give.

In times of stress, you Lord,
  give me the strength and faith to go on.
    You are with me always.
Help me dear Lord to be patient and kind
  when I am tired and my *mother's* needs
  are more than I can cope with.
Still the thoughtless words upon my lips
  and help me to convey warm words of love and comfort.
O God, bless *mother,* and I pray that this night
  may be free of pain and distress.
Help me to meet the night's problems,
    to manage with little sleep;
    to face the new day with a calm heart,
    refreshed and inspired by your presence.
O heavenly Father,
  thank you for periods of remission from pain and distress
  for they bring so much hope and joy.

Help me Lord;
  I feel so disgruntled when family visit *mother,*
  and they do not seem to show concern for me.
Help me to be generous and understanding
  in my thoughts, words and deeds
and may I have no regrets for things I've left undone.

It is so hard Lord to get away for an hour or so.
Help people to see and understand my needs,
    to be not afraid to sit with the sick
    and to realise my need of company in the evening hours.
O God the Creator of the world,
  thank you for the healing peace of nature.
I walked in the garden at dusk
  and the beauty of your creation filled my heart and restored my will
    to continue.
Lord hear my prayer.

Gone — slammed the door

He's gone!
   Slammed the door,
     and says
       he never wants to see me again.
   How did we get into this mess?
   Why did we all say such destructive things?

Father we are truly concerned for . . . .
   and worried what *he* might do right now.
Protect *him* we pray
   and restore us all to a sense of calm
   in which we can think clearly and act sensibly.

We ask for the gift of your love
   that understanding and reconciliation may be possible;
Hear us Lord.

Losing love and joy

Merciful God, bless we pray
   those whose marriage is losing
   the love and joy that once was theirs.

Awaken in them the desire
   to recognise and overcome the problems
     that face them now.
Grant that in your strength and love
   they may rediscover each other and grow together;
   through Jesus Christ our Saviour.

We're separated now . . .

We're separated now . . .
Everloving God,
   grant me the strength to face each new day,
   to live each minute in the knowledge that you are with me.
   Help me to hear your voice and be guided by you.
   When I'm talking to my *wife*
      give me the words that will lovingly show *her*
      that I want to understand
      what's causing the trouble between us.
   May we keep the communications going as we sort out our differences.
   Give me tolerance Lord,
      and help me to know that you love us both.

I thank thee for the wonderful years we shared
– a widow prays

God our Father, I thank thee for all the wonderful years that . . . . . . and I
   shared.
I remember the joys and the sorrows.
I thank thee that thou art my comforter and guide, and will never leave me
   nor forsake me. Through my loneliness help me always to know that
   thou wilt be with me, strengthening me to know without a doubt, that
   "there is no separation in the realms of love."
I pray that I may always live up to my loved one's expectation of me and
   do thy will; all this I ask through Jesus Christ our Lord.

I'm alone

Lord Jesus, the service is over,
   the people have gone
      and I'm alone;
   alone with the memories,
   alone with the hurt
     as if I'm cut in half.
How will I cope Lord?
   My children won't know their *father*.
     It's all so empty.

And yet Lord
   I saw that glimpse of hope and assurance,
     you don't forsake us,
     you embrace all people,
     you look at us with loving eyes,
     you share this pain.
Thank you for ....
Thank you for everything we had,
   for the gift of life you gave us.
Thank you for our children
   and time of growth and happiness.
Help me to remember your promise of eternal life,
   and that everything we are
   and that everything we have
   comes through God our Father.
You love us more than we can possibly imagine.
Thank you for this
   and for your strength
   as I take the first steps of living again.

Why are we here – a prayer of a mother in court

Why are we here Lord?
Where did I go wrong?
Was I too strict?
Did I overindulge?

The experts say you must communicate.
  I thought we did.
  Yet – the pull of *his* peers is so strong.

I see the people going before the judge;
  we sit – waiting our turn;
  where are the other parents?

He looks at me – a nervous smile.
He knows I'm here – that I'm nervous too.
Our eyes meet – it's all right,
  we're in this together for good and bad.

Thank you Lord for holding us together.

My *wife* was an alcoholic

God of compassion,
  thank you for giving me strength and courage
  when I had the problem of living with an alcoholic;
  strength to seek help from others who knew this problem;
  courage to know that I was a problem too
    in my over-protective and critical ways.
  Thank you for their understanding fellowship and help,
        for my deepening faith in you,
        for the gift of patience and trust
      until my *wife* recovered from *her* sickness.
Sustainer of us all,
  help others as you have helped me;
  help me to meet others in their need.

Lord, I hate him

Lord I am afraid —
    take my fear and turn it into safety,

Lord I am sad —
    take my sorrow and turn it into joy,

Lord I am powerless —
    take my powerlessness and turn it into strength,

Lord I am desperate —
    take my despair and turn it into hope,

Lord I hate him —
    take my hate and turn it into love,

                Help me Lord.

He hit me again today

He hit me again today —
I am hurting;
    but the physical pain is almost unimportant
    compared to the hurt in my stomach,
                in my chest.

Lord you promised to set me free but
    I feel trapped;
        trapped by the power he has over me,
        trapped by my loyalty to him,
        trapped by my own pride.
    May he find someone
        to help him face up to what he is doing
        to me and the children.
    Grant me
        the wisdom to act for the good of us all,
        the patience to treat him in a caring way.

Lord God, through Jesus
  you know the power and pain of human cruelty;
  come into our lives,
  bring your love and wisdom to us,
  touch us with the power of your
    healing and reconciling presence.

Lord, why did they break in?

Lord, why did they come?
      Why did they break?
      Why did they enter?
      Why did they choose us?
      Why did they ransack?
      Why! Why! Why!

We've worked so hard to make our home
  a place of welcome,
  a place of caring,
  a place of sanctuary,
  but in a moment it seems destroyed.

God of Creation,
  calm me now,
  strengthen me now to recreate our home.
Help me too, to take my part
  to recreate our community,
  that your kingdom may come
  in earth as it is in heaven.

Baby's still crying!

Baby's still crying!
She's been howling forever it seems!
I want to pick *her* up and shake *her*,
   shake *her* till *she* stops,
     even stops for ever!

Loving Father,
   help me in my frustration,
          my anger,
          my helplessness,
          my aloneness,
     to be a good *mother,*
     to cope with this overwhelming
       responsibility of parenthood.
   Give me the courage to ask for help
     and support from those around me.
   Give me the strength not to turn
     my anger against my child.
   Grant me the peace
     that can break through
       my darkest moments,
       my total aloneness.

Protect my child from violence

God of peace,
    take away this anger in me.
        Calm me Lord.

    Give me your gentleness;
        allow me to be your instrument of love
        not this vehicle of violence.

    Protect my child from all violence
        especially mine.

    Bring compassion in to my heart
        so that I can overcome my feelings of anger
        and of worthlessness.
    Give me the courage to find help.

Lord you love me
    even in these moments of despair.

        Calm me Lord.

Thank You

Enrich our lives with creative beauty

Christ Jesus, at your carpenter's bench
   you knew the joy and fulfilment
   of creating with your hands.
We thank you for our hands,
   the skills you have given us
   and the opportunities to care in your name.
Enrich our lives with the creative beauty
   given to us by those with special talents;
   may we and they acknowledge always
   that these are your gifts of creation.

My baby is due

Loving Father thank you
   for your gift to us
   of this new life within me.
Thank you that you know all about this child
   and I pray that *she* will grow
   to love and serve you;
   in Jesus' name.

For the blessings of our marriage — thank you

Almighty Father we thank you
    for the many blessings you have given us through marriage;
    for the happiness and love that have been ours;
    for the growth you have made possible in each of us as people;
    for the new dimensions which you bring to our love
        through joys, and through sorrows shared.
We pray that we may never take one another for granted
    but may continually be renewed by your grace;
    and we offer the future
        for you to bless;
    through Jesus Christ our Saviour.

It all came right today

Thank you loving God
    for guiding us through this difficult time in our lives;
    for being always with us
        even when we felt it hard to find your presence.

Today it has all come right
    and we are joyful
    in the knowledge that our hopes and prayers
    have been answered in your way.
We rededicate our lives to you and to your service,
    confirmed and strengthened in our faith;
    in the name of Jesus.

My God, I am trusting in you

My God,
   now and always
   I am trusting in you.
   As the sun and the air,
     the soil and the rain
       nourish the summer rose,
  so I feel peace and health,
     strength and control
       flowing through me.
For these bountiful gifts of your goodness
  to take and to share,
     I thank you Lord.
     I am revitalised.
     I am filled with God.
     I can do all things
       through Jesus Christ.

Thank you

Heavenly Father, I thank you for my life,
  for the many good things you have given me;
    my health and strength,
    the ability to walk and talk,
    to see and hear without difficulty.
I thank you for the knowledge
  that you are always there for me;
  that no matter what I do,
    I can still turn back to you
    with repentance in my heart.
But most of all
  I thank you for your everlasting love
    and protection over me;
    in Jesus' name I pray.

Night and Day

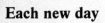

Each new day

Let me pause as I begin this new day
   to give it to you Lord.
Before the tumult of activities breaks in;
   before breakfast plates crash through my still sleepy mind;
     for this last moment in my bed,
        thank you Lord.

Let me hold your promise of new life.
Keep me from slipping back
   for I know that what is forgiven
     is as if it never were.

Each new day,
   your grace gives me a fresh start
     to walk in your light again.

Night Time

Thank you God
    for the balance of day and night
    for the comfort and warmth of our beds;
    for unbroken nights in fresh sheets;
    for changes in attitudes that refreshing sleep brings;
    for your care and love continuing through the night.

Remind us Lord, of those
    sleeping in the streets — rejected,
    tossing through hospital nights,
    sitting alone by dying relations;
        insomniacs who dread these dark hours,
        children frightened by drunken fights,
        mothers helplessly watching
            ill or starving children;
    those with fears magnified
        by the intensity of darkness,
    the lonely, the sick, the disturbed,
    the outcasts of society,
        who in our comfort we easily forget.

Use us Lord,
    join our prayers with those of countless others
        to spread your love
        and to ease the sufferings beyond our imaginings
        for which we must share responsibility.